THE
GLASSMAKER
Discovering the Impact of Vision

Shenay Shumake

1

The Glassmaker: Discovering the Impact of Vision

ISBN 13: 978-0-578-61162-4

Flette and Nay Publishing

CONTENTS

DEDICATION

::::::::::

Mom, Thank you for putting a sheet of paper and a pencil in my 3-year-old hands and telling me to, **"Write."**

Thank you for giving me a Bible and concordance and telling me to **"Read."**

Thank you for being a consistent model that taught me to **"Pray."**

FOREWORD

::::::::::

Admittedly, this book is about more than just having a vision. This book is also about the quality of the vision you have. Perhaps you're reading it because you've never really thought much about having a personal vision. Maybe you're reading this book because you have already had a vision. I'd like you to consider the upcoming chapters as an assessment for creating a vision or expanding your view. I hope that you'd go beyond what you thought was possible and reasonable. After you've read this book, you may discover your vision is too small. I invite you to look again.

I hope that you'd be willing to look inside the Father's heart for the dream that rested there as you slept in your mother's womb. Just like the prophet Jeremiah, chosen, known, and ordained in his mother's womb, you, too, were born into a purpose and a destiny. (Jeremiah 1:1)

Our future picture lives in the kind of

intention of our Heavenly Father's will for our lives. It is my prayer that you will see what needs creating, deconstructing, and what needs color, form, and dimension, and you'll do your part to upgrade your Vision. Trusting that God is doing His part to help you recapture and reclaim the Great Beauty that God desires to produce from your life.

CHAPTER ONE
Meet Bernie the Glassmaker

::::::::::

On the other side of the world near the deep blue waters of the Adriatic Sea, in the Lagoon of Venice, is the Italian island of Murano. On that island have lived many exciting people, but none as fascinating as Bernardo Salomon.

Bernardo, known as Bernie to his friends, looked ordinary. He was old, stout, and wrinkled with thinning hair and a sallow complexion. Bernie sported a larger than average nose, thin lips, and reliable hands. His eyebrows were slight tufts of fur that grew into one long brow. Perhaps Bernie's best feature was his eyes: deep puddles of warm chocolate brown that sparkled and danced by the light of the fire. Though Bernie looked ordinary, he was extraordinary, and his eyes made him unforgettable.

Bernie's eyes were memorable not just because they always seemed to twinkle, but because of what they saw. Now, Bernie's eyesight wasn't the keenest. He had worn spectacles for as long as he could remember. But Bernie was known for having great insight. He could look at the plainest and crudest of things and see its potential. He could gaze at anyone and anything and see the power of what could be. Bernie had a great vision, and his passion was making great beauty.

Some of the villagers in Murano might rise while it was still night, to catch fish to sell when the market opened at dawn. Some were gondoliers-- water taxi drivers ferrying visitors along the canals of Venice. Others worked the salt mines. None of these things ever interested, Bernie. Bernie never rose before dawn to do anything but create great beauty.

Bernie was a glassmaker and not just any glassmaker—he was the world's premier glassmaker. Local villagers, taking pride in his beautiful work, never hesitated to remind tourists that the world's best glassmakers had apprenticed for Bernie. Logically, this made Bernie the "best of the best." Bernie became a legend, and it all began with what he saw—and what he did with what he saw.

Murano, known for its glassmakers for centuries, and glassmaking was the Salomon family trade. In Bernie's day, many glassmakers never left Murano. Passion kept them bound to their workrooms: they possessed a noble desire for keeping their families well-fed, and for offering beauty and functionality to the world. Their beautiful creations saw and served the world, while they never left Murano. Lamps and lanterns hung from trembling hands and towering edifices. Gorgeous basins blessed new babies, and Popes drank communion wine from ornate glass goblets.

Bernie's grandfather had been an excellent glassmaker. He handed down the craft to his only son, who, in his turn, taught the art to Bernie. But Bernie's father did not love glassmaking. To him, it was merely an obligation, not a passion—and it showed in the quality of his work. Few people wanted to buy the creations of an uninspired craftsman, so business was terrible for the Salomon family. Bernie grew up poor, and his father eventually died penniless and bitter. As he lay upon his deathbed, Bernie's father pulled him near and whispered through his parched lips, "Don't be a glassmaker. It's difficult and pays poorly. Get out and see the world, or you'll be miserable, just like me." And with that, he breathed his last breath.

Days later, Bernie kissed his mother goodbye and left Murano to obey his father's dying request. Against the urging of his friends, he went to see the world. He traveled far and wide.

On his own, Bernie found life difficult. The more he traveled, the more he saw. The more he saw, the more he wanted. Wanting so much but having so little was heart-wrenching. Bernie worked and traveled, scraping out a living however he could. Eventually, he found a job that brought him enough money to afford those things he had seen and wanted. For a while, Bernie was satisfied—but as time passed by, Bernie discovered that having things was not bringing lasting joy. Instead, he would lie down every night with the sinking, nagging feeling that something was missing. Bernie lived this existence for many long and painful years.

Glassmaking was what had given Bernie joy and satisfaction. It was the best use of his life. Following his father's advice was not. He wanted desperately not to be miserable like his father. At night, when he rested, and his mind was quiet, his heart would speak. He could not elude the yearning of his heart—not even in his dreams.

While others dreamed in black and white, Bernie dreamed of colors. Vivid, mind-blowing color. Fiery reds, deep purples and browns, luscious greens, juicy oranges, tantalizing sun-kissed yellows, and an ocean of blues. Exquisite creations of rare beauty lived—no, danced in his dreams. They were things that he had never seen in all his travels. They were things that he dared to believe no eye had ever seen—a kind of beauty others would crave, a type of beauty that would lift hearts. He longed to bring this beauty to life. Yet he continued the way that he always had, working all day, tossing all night, and dreaming beautiful dreams.

Bernie met glassmakers now and then and tried his best to describe what he saw in his dreams, but none of them could replicate his visions. They all seemed to lack passion. Bernie would leave their shops disappointed and frustrated.

Bernie's dreams became more and more of a nuisance until, finally, he admitted that following his father's advice wasn't working. He was miserable, just as his father had been. To the delight of his friends, he returned to Murano to make glass.

It was the best decision of his life. Every year, Bernie's glass was more beautiful than the year before. Apprentices and rivals pondered what Bernie's secret could be. Some competitors even masqueraded as apprentices, trying to discover why Bernie was the best of the best. His materials were the same as every other glassmaker, gritty white sand, and lots of heat. His tools were nothing to brag about, just decades-old rods, blowing pipes and pliers. His technique was standard. But what he did with those things, what he created, was in a league of its own.

What made the difference? Bernie possessed the incredible power of vision. He refused to waste his talent or effort, producing anything that didn't look like the great beauty that lived in his dreams. In well over 40 years, he did not forget a single dream; he harnessed the power of what he'd seen to create things of beauty.

Bernie began each day the same way. Waking up with a dream in his heart, he would bend his knees beside his bed, give thanks to the Dream Giver, grab his glasses, down his espresso, chomp some biscotti, and head to work to craft his dream.

As time passed, Bernie's reputation grew— along with his wealth. People paid large sums of money for his works of art. They were common things: a simple washbasin, a water pitcher, a drinking glass, a vase for flowers, but elevated to a degree of unrivaled beauty. That's what Bernie did. He made things that people needed and wanted. He made beautiful things that enhanced the way others lived.

Life was perfect for Bernie. He had his art, he had his friends, he gave others beauty and made money doing what he loved the most.

One morning Bernie awoke eager to begin creating beauty. As always, in his heart, there was a fantastic dream, something he had seen while he rested. Every morning, he rolled out of bed and to his knees to say, "Thank you," as he had done every morning. He reached for his glasses as he had done every morning. But this time, for the first time in over 40 years, they were not there. He reached a little further. Still no eyeglasses. He looked on the bed and around the bed, he looked all over his room.

He searched around the kitchen as he sipped his espresso and crunched his biscotti. He checked in his washroom, in his workroom, in his garden. He spent so much time looking that dawn turned to noon, noon to midday, midday to evening and evening tonight. Bernie went to bed.

The next morning Bernie rolled out of bed and scratched his head. Yes, there was a dream in his heart. He could not remember yesterday's dream: he had gone to bed sad the night before because, for the first time in 40 years, he had not created what he dreamed.

Bernie shook his head, shuddering at the thought that today could be anything like yesterday. Out of habit, he reached for his glasses--which, of course, were still missing. He drank his espresso and ate his biscotti, wondering where they could be. Abruptly, he decided that he could not let another dream go to waste. He headed to the workroom. With his tools in his hands, he began to blow and spin his glass.

Days without his glasses turned to weeks, and Bernie continued to do what he had always done. But things were different. Yes, he was productive; he created something every day. But he was so driven by his desire to be productive that he failed to realize that what he was making looked vastly different from the objects in his dreams.

His friends would drop in to see him and ask where his spectacles were. "Somewhere around the house. Maybe in the studio," he'd reply. He wasn't worried. He had watched generations of men in his family shuffle around the furnace room, spinning and blowing intricate creations. He didn't need glasses to know what he was doing. After all, he had held the same tools in his hands most of his life. He was a skilled craftsman and artisan. He was the "best of the best." Even when friends hinted that his work was beginning to look, well, "different," he never told them his glasses had were lost.

He knew his vision was slightly skewed, but he had no idea to what degree. He adjusted—small adjustments every day. He would squint and stare for just a moment longer until his eyes focused enough to continue. Bernie could not see that what he thought was his best work was his worst. What he thought was beauty was only mediocrity.

It was a full six months before Bernie noticed that the shop door seldom opened. He had a few regular customers, but they didn't buy Bernie's glass because he was the best of the best anymore; they bought it out of loyalty. Other customers were not so loyal. For the first time in Bernie's glassmaking career, he had more glass than places to put it.

Bernie had plenty of money but missed the frequent company. Most of all, he missed knowing that he had brightened someone else's life with beauty.

It no longer made sense to create objects every day. There was no place to put them. No one wanted them. His dreams had once again become a nuisance. It was impossible to keep pace with them now. Days of not creating beauty turned into weeks, then months.

Bernie had told his customers and friends about his dreams before. They always listened, fascinated, as Bernie spoke with enthusiasm and passion—usually while holding one of his dream pieces in his hand. He would expound on how he applied copper and cobalt for the most beautiful aquamarine. He explained why he had elongated a specific curve, or why he made the dip of a specific bowl so shallow. He talked about how one vase caught the moonlight and spread rays as it sat on a shelf near the window. In his dreams, that vase had sparkled so brilliantly that it seemed as if rays of light shot from it. Bernie's stories had warmed them. And now he had nothing to say.

One day, Bernie reached the end of his rope and convinced himself all was lost. His talent, his gift, his ability to produce great beauty had finally left him, or so he thought, He was too old. It was time to let go of his dreams — time to close shop and turn off the furnace.

A glassmaker's furnace burns as long as he is alive. Turning off a glassmaker's kiln signifies both the end of existence and the end of a contribution to the world. Bernie's furnace had been burning for over 40 years. The smoke from his fire could be seen from the Adriatic Sea, billowing up and lacing into the clouds.

Bernie, with great tears in his eyes, made his way to the workroom to begin the process of shutting down his furnace. It was the saddest day of his life. He wept so bitterly that he didn't see his friend Vittorio standing before him. Bernie was sobbing so loudly he hadn't heard him come in. He didn't realize Vittorio was there until he felt a gentle hand on his shoulder.

Vittorio, alarmed at Bernie's tears, demanded that Bernie share with him once and for all everything that ailed him. Right there in that hot workroom, with the furnace still smoldering, Bernie began to share what had happened.

In between tears, Bernie told him of all the unsold glass that now filled his shop and how people no longer found great beauty in what he offered. He told him about how he seldom made glass anymore and how his dreams were few and far between. "My days as a glassmaker are over," said Bernie. "And it's time I shut down my furnace. As Bernie shared his story of heartbreak and pain, he mentioned to Vittorio that his troubles began after he lost his glasses.

At that point, Bernie's dear friend began laughing. At first, it was a slight chuckle; it then grew to an irreverent roar.

Bernie was stunned. This longtime friend feigned concern and seemed to make a mockery of Bernie's hardship.

Bernie was so disappointed in Vittorio that he could not even speak. His lip trembled, and he felt weak. What would he do without glassmaking and his friend? He certainly couldn't be expected to continue in friendship with someone so insensitive.

Just as Bernie was beginning to protest, his friend interrupted. "Bernie," Vittorio said, "You have not lost your dreams, and you have not lost your talent. You have lost your vision!"

It wasn't long before Vittorio found Bernie's glasses. They had been under his bed all along. Bernie felt foolish, but he was very grateful to have them back. The first thing he did was survey his work. Just as his friends had said, it was mediocre. Bernie quickly ran to the furnace to add coal, shuddering at the thought of what he had almost done just a half-hour before.

What a joy it was to have his vision restored! Bernie was so excited that he was able to offer the world beauty once again. He still possessed great talent, and his tools were nearby. And Bernie now realized his biggest mistake was not losing his eyeglasses, but in searching for them alone. All he had needed was a friend who could see clearly. If only he had shared the real problem, he would have found his glasses so much sooner and saved himself a lot of heartaches.

Bernie rolled out of bed the next morning with dreams in his heart. With his glasses in place and falling to his knees, Bernie thanked the Dream Giver and Vision Restorer.

CHAPTER TWO
You Have Glass to Make

::::::::::

"For we are his workmanship, created in Christ Jesus for good works, which God prepared beforehand, that we should walk in them." (Ephesians 2:10 ESV)

#

Here are a few things you should know. Bernie is a fictitious character. His story is an allegory. Most of us don't make glass as our occupation. (Although, glassmakers are very cool.) We are, however, "makers" because The Maker created us.

God is a Craftsmen and Master Artist who prolifically writes and speaks unforgettable words. His spoken word solo performance weaved an expansive, provocative, and sensorial world. He sketched every living thing and handcrafted humanity in His image. When we look around us, it's evident that there's no end to the brilliant imagination of God...and we are His image. We were made to make something. We weren't made to be a mess or make a mess, and we were created to produce good works.

You were born to make something. You have a brand of glass that the world will clamor to obtain. Your glass is your God-given purpose, your reason for existence, and your highest contribution to the world. It is what gives God glory, satisfies you, and what causes you to work hard. For me, it's writing and speaking words that are refreshing to others. I leap on the inside when I have an idea about something to say or something to write. It's what I'd rather be doing, most days. I am so sure that this is my glass. I'm not sure what your "glass" is, but I know once produced, it will be globally prized for its beauty. Because every glassmaker has a desire to make beautiful glass.

I know God loves beauty. I think authors Jon and Stasi Eldridge says it best in their book *Captivating*, "Nature is not primarily functional. It is primarily beautiful. Stop for a minute and let that sink in. We're so used to evaluating everything and (everyone) by their usefulness that this thought will take a minute or two to begin to dawn on us. Nature is not primarily functional; it is primarily beautiful. Which is to say, beauty is in and of itself great and gloriously good, something we need in large and daily doses."[1]

If your life is primarily functional and void of beauty, it's time to get some glasses and see God and your life through heaven's perspective. A clearer picture of the nature of God and some clarity about your purpose positions you to know that you are beautiful and made for exceptional beauty. Producing Great Beauty is how we glorify God. One definition of glory is "great beauty." God has made us for His glory or His great beauty.

"Bring all who claim me as their God, for I have made them for my glory. It was I who created them." (Isaiah 43:7)

Essentially, God is saying He created us, we

---

[1]. Eldredge, John. Captivating: Unveiling the Mystery of a Woman's Soul, Keepsake Edition. Nashville, TN: Thomas Nelson, 2007.

belong to Him, and we are made for something beautiful. And when we offer great beauty from what He makes of our lives, it is our big thank you to God! After all, God first created a beautiful world. He created a beautiful garden in the center, and beautiful creatures to live there. God put us in the center of that lovely garden to occupy it. Our first earthly environment was one of great beauty and divine order. That's why we crave beauty. There is a need to have it all around us, to taste it, touch it, smell it, and see it. We desperately long for our lives to match the beauty that we crave. God has put in every human being a "need" for beauty and the ability to produce it when we make the glass we were designed to make.

No one is exempt; we all have glass to make. Every created thing has a specific intention, not a random function. Genesis paints the picture of God's purpose for every created thing. Everything God creates has a job or responsibility. God created the "sky" whose job was to keep the water in heaven separated from the water on earth. God made two great lights, whose job was to govern the day and the night. God even made humanity and immediately gave him a purpose.

Then God blessed them and said, *"Be fruitful and multiply. Fill the earth and govern it. Reign over the fish in the sea, the birds in the sky, and all the animals that scurry along the ground."* (Genesis 1:28 NLT)

God never has and will never create anything without an intended purpose. God has given humankind the general responsibility to be fruitful, multiply, fill the earth, and govern it. Our "glass" will do this, and it will only produce what is right over and over again, filling the earth. Still, this is very general; each person has the task of defining their "glass." I believe that's where we need Christ's help.

"For you died to this life, and your real life is hidden with Christ in God." (Colossians 3:3 NLT)

Hidden. Maybe the best use of our life is

concealed, secure, and protected, not unlike a buried treasure. Hidden in the work of the cross and our love relationship with Jesus is our specific and intended purpose. Hidden in Christ is our glass, the function that it has, the form that it takes, and the beauty that it conveys. For many of us, it's already there. It just needs to be discovered. It is what we should be doing.

#

I know that I have been asked and have answered that question many times as a kid. My mom would send me in another room, and maybe it was the kitchen to grab her a glass of water. Perhaps I was supposed to go and retrieve something from the car. Simple tasks that should only take a matter of seconds, somehow morphed into minutes and rare occasions, an hour. It was the length of time that I was gone and the eerie quietness in the house that would make my mom stop what she was doing and set off to find me; or sneak up on me, depending on your perspective. She would ask this question of me at various moments of my upbringing and in multiple tones, "What should you be doing?" At times her question was genuinely curious. I would be gone so long she only had an inkling that she had asked me to do something. Other times it was a gentle chiding guiding me back to her original request. And yes, there were times that the question "What should you be doing?" dripped with a stern warning, which made me stop dead in my tracks and get back on track because to delay meant swift discipline.

Many times in my life, I can hear my mother asking, "What should you be doing?" Sometimes in my voice, when I am trying to keep my children focused on the task at hand. And at times in my voice, when I've felt the gentle nudging of the Holy Spirit inviting me to change direction. Still, I have had to ask myself many times, in many phases of my life, "What should you be doing?" The answer to this question has always caused me to make changes. Some changes were drastic, while other changes were incremental. This question is so important because when we answer it with naked honesty, we learn the best use of our lives. I plan on continuing to ask myself this question because I always want to be moving in the direction of God's purpose. So, I ask it of you, and I pray it for myself complete with sincere curiosity, gentle prodding, and stern warning, "What should you be doing?" Making our brand of glass answers the question of what we "should" be doing.

Admittedly, it takes a great deal of courage to divert, especially when it's a lot more comfortable to keep doing whatever it is that you're doing. At some point, diverting may cost you, but choosing to continue creating mediocrity is also charging you, maybe even robbing you of life and fulfillment. If this is the place you find yourself in, it's time to give yourself the gift of really seeing what life is supposed to be.

CHAPTER THREE
There Are No Blind Glassmakers

::::::::::

One thing's for sure; whatever glass you make, you can't make it blind. There are just too many real dangers for a blind glassmaker. The threat of the fire dying, the risk of an uncontained fire. The danger of being badly burned or burned alive by getting too close to the heat. Fire burns and someone who blows glass blind increases the risk of injury exponentially. It wouldn't be prudent.

I'm not writing about physical visual impairment, however, but about being visually impaired spiritually. Helen Keller was born physically blind and deaf, and yet she had more vision than those who could see 20/20. One of my favorite quotes by Helen Keller, "The most pathetic person in the world is someone who has sight but has no vision."[2]

---

[2]. Richards, Norman. *Helen Keller*. Chicago: Children's Press, 1968.

Being able to see but unable to perceive is a great sadness. As an avid moviegoer, I know that a lack of perception can be dangerous. Whenever I arrive late to the movies, it's frustrating because my eyes don't quickly adjust in the dark, and perception becomes a problem. Is that a foot? Or an empty box of popcorn? Is that a seat or a stair? The problem with trying to see in the dark is that in darkness, our relative distance perception and depth perception shifts. We can't tell how close the wall is until we run into it. We don't know that the step is farther away from our foot, so we misstep. It is difficult to do anything when our perception or vision is hindered.

Clear vision is the most critical tool that a Glassmaker has. A Glassmaker needs to see to keep himself and others safe. Still, Glassmakers also need to have great vision and understand its value. Perception is "something seen otherwise than by ordinary eyesight." For a Glassmaker, vision is a compass. When you have sand, heat, and a few metal rods, it takes great vision to blow and spin, not just anything, but a beautiful thing. It's vitally necessary to have a clear future picture of what you want to end up with after all of that blowing and spinning.

Without the compass of vision, glassmakers can't discern the difference between unmatched beauty and mediocrity. The quality of the glass relies on the clarity of the vision.

#

So, what exactly is "vision?" How do we define it beyond physiological terms? I want to begin by saying what vision is not. Vision is not identity. Identity is whose you are and who you are. We are sons and daughters beloved by God. When our life mirrors this truth, it's terrific, but even if our lives don't reflect this truth, we still belong to Him. That's identity.

Vision is also not the same as a purpose. "Purpose" is why you exist. Purpose is specific yet broad enough to have many applications. God-given purpose doesn't live in a boundary of roles, titles, occupations, or opportunities. When our purpose unveils, we can be what we were made to be, regardless of where we are or what we're doing. It is instinctive for fish to swim. They don't wait for permission. It's just what they do because it's what they were born to do. Purpose is natural, intentional, and powerful.

Vision is also not your mission. Mission is your assignment. Mission has elements of place and space, and mission requires performance. If you're a fish and your purpose is to swim, then Mission can be better explained as where you swim and why you swim there. Freshwater or saltwater? Lake or ocean? Mission is the eco-system in which you live out your Purpose and the responsibility that your purpose is meant to carry. So then personal vision is what that eco-system and assignment look like for you. It's what you're building, creating, solving, performing, or crafting based on who you are, what you were born to do, and where you were called to do it. Vision then is not arbitrary; it's systemic and systematic. It's a snapshot of those divine and sacred truths about you and why you exist. And unlike identity, purpose, and mission, which endure throughout lives, vision should have a time limit attached to it. It's supposed to be fulfilled, intended to be accomplished and supposed to happen.

Vision then is a stunning picture of your future, created from a supernatural revelation given by God. And it compels you to run towards its' fulfillment relentlessly. There you have it, a stunning future picture, birthed through revelation, forcing you to run. That's how I define vision. It is also vitally important to have a vision for every dimension of your life. From your health to your home, from your marriage to your money. Vision matters.

Vision as a future picture reveals the beauty of what your life should be, and it endures as a promise of what your life can become. Who you are, where you are, or what you've experienced can't stop you from moving forward if you have a clear vision. Vision is an essential part of the blueprint in creating a life that matches God's dream. When our lives are pale in comparison to the vibrant, detailed color of what thrives in God's heart, it's time to realign our lives. We must dream a bigger dream.

We can think of great things to do. We can lend our talents to noteworthy projects and productive ideas. Still, true fulfillment begins to unfold when we dare to get a revelation of what our life is supposed to be. It's not a process that we can rush. Like a five-star meal and fine wine, it takes time, careful consideration, and some risk expressed through adventure and creativity. My recipe for clarity and expansive vision involves me, alone with God, with a lot of stillness and a lot of beauty. It's an investment that requires me to make space in my calendar and space in my heart, to tune out the noise of social media and quiet the nagging inner critic. I ask a lot of questions as I pray through what more could God want for my life. I listen to God and myself, paying attention to my experiences, my inner longings, and my burdens. I mourn what I've lost and missed, and I celebrate what I've attained. My consistent and necessary cycle of stepping out of knowledge and into God's, upgrades my desires for my life. And I find that I am dreaming dreams that I never thought I would ever imagine. And not only that, I begin to pray prayers that I never thought I would ever pray.

It's in this context, this incubator of possibility, that vision becomes clear enough, loud enough, and good enough to run despite challenges, setbacks, stalls, and obstacles. And when we believe that God's Vision for our life is excellent, we will run towards it instead of hiding from it, knowing that with every step, our legs get stronger. Our hearts beat more passionately for what our lives should be.

Some of us can see a vision so grand that it can make us run in the opposite direction. It's essential to make a U-turn and trust God because what God sees for us is always so much better than what we can see and dream for ourselves. What God sees has always served us more than what we see without Him.

#

Imagine that a nation is lost, broken, and apart from God. Injustice and violence prevail. One man, a prophet, continually looks at the strife and conflict. In his hopelessness, he believes that the law is paralyzed. He petitions to God. The man is the prophet Habakkuk, and the nation is Israel.

"Why do you make me look at injustice? Why do you tolerate wrongdoing? Destruction and violence are before me; there is strife, and conflict abounds. Therefore, the law is paralyzed, and justice never prevails. The wicked hem in the righteous so that justice is perverted." (Habakkuk 1:3-4 NIV)

God answers Habakkuk's first complaint about the wickedness of His people, assuring him that he would raise the Babylonians as a punishment. Later, Habakkuk still in distress laments at the brutality of the Babylonians towards God's people. The terror of the Babylonians is so ferocious, and Habakkuk feels that the situation is so grave he wonders aloud to God,

"Will you let them get away with this forever? Will they succeed forever in their heartless conquests?" (Habakkuk 1:17 NLT)

Habakkuk then "waits" to see what God would say. In his hopelessness, despair, fear, and dread, he is expectantly waiting for God to give him his answer. God gives a startling response to Habakkuk's lament.

"Record the vision And inscribe it on tablets, That the one who reads it may run. For the vision is yet for the appointed time; It hastens toward the goal, and it will not fail. Though it tarries, wait for it; For it will certainly come, it will not delay." (Habakkuk 2:3 NASB)

Amid the gravest of circumstances, God instructs Habakkuk to write down the "future picture" of what he wants to do for His people. Whenever we are at ground zero, there is always a future picture, and it is God's picture. God still whispers a word to us and paints a picture for us because His intention for us remains unscathed amidst tragedy and despair. Vision, the critical matter of life and death that God uses like jumper cables, to shock us back when we lie listless and unresponsive.

Maintaining vision at the forefront of our lives is crucial; because vision is always the first thing, that struggle will attack. Michael Hyatt renowned speaker, blogs, "When times are tough, vision is the first casualty."[3] Preserving personal vision is a vigilant and consistent battle that we will fight at various times in life. Still, in winning the war on mediocrity, vision must be heavily guarded.

It's so important that we remain convinced of Vision's essentiality. God implies the necessity of vision as he commands Habakkuk to write down the future picture. It's almost as if the vision that Habakkuk writes, prompted by God, is the

---

[3] Michael Hyatt. "Why Vision Is More Important Than Strategy." Michael Hyatt, August 12, 2012. https://michaelhyatt.com/why-vision-is-more-important-than-strategy/.

guarantee to Habakkuk that God will intervene and that His intervention is to Israel's advantage. God is so determined to give Israel a better future that he tells Habakkuk to record at this moment what He wants to do for his people in the next. Then he adds an invitation for Habakkuk to believe the future picture.

"Behold, his soul is puffed up; it is upright within him, but righteous shall live by his faith." (Habakkuk 2:4)

Habakkuk's record of the future picture inspires hope in him, and his response is optimistic in spite of what it looks like now,

Vision is still the undeniable difference-maker. Seeing, embracing, and writing vision remains the starting point for offering great beauty. Dare to write down what you see for your future. Write it, descriptively, so that when it happens, you can mark the moment and have receipts.

#

A beautiful life is a receipt for a promise that you believed. A promise rooted in the love of God with a destination in the future and Great Beauty is attainable when we say, "Yes and Amen." to vision. The best glass, the best life we can ever create, is foundational to vision. Clear sight allows us to develop a discerning eye. When we are discerning glassmakers, we look carefully at what we produce. When you have a discerning eye, you can tell a reproduction from the real thing.

Knowing our talents, passion, and purpose, will cause us to require excellence of ourselves. But when we have a Great Vision, we're able to produce the excellence that we can see. When we can see clearly and unencumbered, we can create Great Beauty. Bernie's story emphasizes that critical fact. It teaches us the high value of vision.

Vision has incalculable value, and the quality of your vision is just as important as having a vision at all. Over the next few chapters, we'll look at six qualities of the kind of vision that produces Great

Beauty. It's not enough to see, but we must see well, because when we possess Great Vision, we own more than just a great perspective. When we have a vision inspired by God's heart and our plea, we have a picture of what life is supposed to be like, which causes us to grow restless with anything less than that picture.

Our Vision should be clear, unclouded, and unobstructed. It should be fervent, blazing with a white-hot passion and intensity. It should be focused, singular in its' intention, divine in its origin, successful in its aim and eternal in its reach.

A vision shouldn't take our limitations into account. Neither should it audit our assets. Vision is supposed to solve problems, inspire awe, push our limits, threaten our comfort, and be too much for us to manage on our own. If your vision is neatly contained or easily handled, perhaps it's just a goal with colorful language and maybe it's time to look again.

In 2018, my husband and I went to the Vatican and saw for ourselves the Sistine Chapel. It took my breath away because I had always only seen bits and pieces of it in history books and on blogs. It wasn't until I was there, that I could see that the Sistine Chapel is several vignettes that formed a larger story. The finger of God not only touching humanity, or Eve holding the apple in the Eden with Adam, it is from beginning to end, a sequential picture of God's redemptive work through the cross of Jesus Christ. This story is told in "snapshots." Our story, too, is described in snapshots. Vision vignette's that give us a glimpse of the bigger picture, what God can redeem in us, for us, with us, and through us. That's what a Great Vision points to—the result of redemption. And it's made possible when we learn how to see.

CHAPTER FOUR
Clear Vision Sharpens Community

::::::::::

Sometimes we can't see alone. We see partially or dimly but seeing with others increases our scope of vision and our reach, therefore, Great Vision is sharpened, in the context of Great Community.

Bernie was blessed to have a community of friends who shared his dreams. They were the people who listened with anticipation while he shared the Great Beauty of his dreams. His friends were supporters who recognized the best use of Bernie's life even before Bernie. They celebrated Bernie's return home, were Bernie's patrons, and provided Bernie with the love and companionship every human being craves. Bernie's community was the first to notice when Bernie wasn't quite himself. They were the ones who searched out Bernie's broken heartedness. It was Bernie's friend who helped Bernie recover his sight. Good communities only make us better.

We are created for community, connecting with God, and others. Community, after all, is God's idea. It was God, who said,

"... It is not good for man to be alone; I will make him a helper fit for him." (Genesis 3:18)

It was God that made Adam a helper suitable for him. God loves the community. It's no wonder that community or "common unity" is the context for blessing and life forever. (Psalms 133:1)

As an individual, maybe we don't have all the pieces of the puzzle. Alone, we lack skills and resources, but what's missing can be found in the community.

Only God is a multi-directional visionary. We merely see parts of the whole, the aerial view or the ground, rarely do we see the middle portion. We see what's in front, but not behind us or beside us. We see our present lives, but strain to look into the future. We need the eyes of the community to bring clarity to what we see and to point out what has escaped our scrutiny. Great Vision grows all the sharper in Great Community.

Even the worst ideas can come alive in the collective unity of vision. The Tower of Babel illustrates for us what can happen when we all say and see the same thing.

#

"Now the whole earth had one language and the same words. And as people migrated from the east, they found a plain in the land of Shinar and settled there. And they said to one another, 'Come, let us build ourselves a city and a tower with its top in the heavens, and let us make a name for ourselves, lest we are dispersed over the face of the whole earth.' And the Lord came down to see the city and the tower, which the children of man had built And the Lord said, 'Behold, they are one people, and they have all one language, and this is only the beginning of what they will do. And nothing that they propose to do will not be impossible for them..." (Genesis 11:1-6)

The impossible is made possible because of our shared vision and focus. The most seemingly ridiculous and unfathomable dreams are conceived when we see them together.

Let's take a look at Bernie once again. If Bernie had shared with his community of friends that he had lost his vision, (eyeglasses), they would have been eager to help him find them. He would have found his glasses a lot sooner and saved himself a lot of heartache and pain. Great Community has the power to find solutions, recover what's lost, and do more with less. A great community can also help you go higher and grow faster than you could alone.

Consider the early church in the book of Acts. It was the fastest-growing church in all of history. It grew by a few thousand each day. As if that were not enough of a miracle, these people had all things in common. In the biblical context, it means more than just selling the possessions that they had and giving these resources to be distributed to all. It was sharing their very lives.

As leaders or parents, we understand the

enormous challenge to get people to share, let alone a single idea. Imagine thousands selling what they had, sleeping, dreaming, eating, and advancing in tandem. The early church increased because of the Gospel, the Holy Spirit, and the collective unity of Vision. Thousands upon thousands made an impact on billions upon billions, generations upon generations later because of what they dared to see, together.

They dared to see together that Jesus was the Christ! This common Vision enabled them to see more clearly and compelled them to call a stranger, brother.

Great Community sees more than externally. Great Community also helps us to see inwardly. Great Community sees the bits that we overlook when our successes and failures distract us. It was Bernie's friend who drew attention to a critical fact that Bernie considered a minor detail. Those friends in Great Community are the people that we've permitted to share dreams with us. They are our "attaboys."

"And Nathan said to the king, "Go do all that is in your heart, for the Lord is with you." (II Samuel 7:3)

They are also the ones that show us how we've missed the mark when we've gotten a little too big for our britches.

"...Why have you despised the word of the Lord to do what was evil in his sight?" (II Samuel 12:9)

Every person needs the kind of community that Nathan was for David. We would be destined to live sub-par lives if the people who live in Great Community with us don't permit us to go after our dreams and don't dare to show us what we need to see to get our lives back on track.

Most importantly, the masters knew full well, and any glassmaker the world over will readily confirm; that considering the state of the art at that time, it is absurd to believe that anyone, can merely observe how glass is made and proceed to teach the process to others.

"To master the art of glassmaking," the

practitioners of the art declare, winking shrewdly, "it is essential to obtain a great-grandfather who was a master!"

They are the ones who love us enough to tell us the truth. They are the ones who are willing to stand between our disappointed selves and what we'll almost do because of what we no longer see. These, living in Great Community with us, are the ones God uses to restore lost vision and to redirect vision that has somehow strayed.

Have you given others the freedom to see with you, and have you permitted them to bring greater clarity to what you see? Inviting Great Community to see with you can mean the difference between throwing in the towel and realizing real success. Wisely choose Vision partners to help you achieve the Great Beauty of your dreams in an important part of what clear vision can do.

VISION NOT is identity

-Shenay Shumake

CHAPTER FIVE
Fervent Vision Enlists Support

::::::::::

He dared to stand in the King's presence with his face sad and his heart heavy. His name was Nehemiah, a Jew taken to Babylon in the exile and cupbearer to the King of Persia. A trusted confidant. It was Nehemiah's role in the court of King Artaxerxes I to keep the king safe by preventing anyone from poisoning his cup. Suffice it to say, that the King trusted Nehemiah with his very life.

Several years after the Jews had returned from captivity in Babylon, Nehemiah's brother Hanani comes to visit him. Nehemiah inquires about the Jews who have returned to the city, and upon learning that the people are lying in ruins, he begins to fast and pray for months. Andy Stanley, author of *Visioneering: God's Blueprint for Developing and Maintaining Personal Vision*, says, "Prayer keeps the burden fresh. It keeps our eyes and hearts in an expectant mode."[4] Nehemiah is in an expectant mode and finally sees an opportunity to enlist support from the King.

He petitions God to give him favor with King Artaxerxes and eventually enlists the King's support and returns to Jerusalem with letters from the King, resources from the King, and the King's troops for protection. When he returns to Jerusalem, he mobilizes the very people who are living in ruins to build. And that's exactly what the people do—they build. They eventually built the wall and completed it though not without opposition. Still, the opposition didn't keep them from finishing the wall that had laid waste for over a decade, completing it in only 52 days!

Nehemiah had an intense vision, birthed in the context of fervent prayer and fasting. What begins as a request and a burden became the solution and a brilliant picture of what was possible

---

[4]. Stanley, Andy. Visioneering - God's Blueprint for Developing and Maintaining Vision. Multnomah Press, 2005.

as he fervently prayed. And the picture that he saw became so white-hot, so alive, so real, and so plausible that he was eventually willing to risk his life to enlist support for it. In the process of a burden becoming a vision, Nehemiah, developed a strategy that included getting help from the King. Nehemiah challenges me because he sacrifices his comfort for those who are living in gross discomfort, and he uses his influence to help people understand their capacity.

Every big vision needs enormous support. And, we must enlist this support by asking for it. Sometimes we make excuses and tell ourselves that we need a big bang to involve ourselves with a cause that sacrifices our own comfort. Nehemiah is unique in that he doesn't have an announcement from heaven to get out of his father's house like Abram. (Genesis 12:1) He doesn't have a burning bush moment like Moses. (Exodus 3:3) No one strikes him down and strikes him blind like Saul. (Acts 9:4-6) None of these things happened in

Nehemiah's case, and he still partners with God to realize a Vision for the Jews that was part of God's promise to them. You don't need a dream or a sign to honor the burdens in your heart. You need to pray them through until they burn white-hot, and you can see not just what is, but what can be. And when it comes to a Great Vision, what can be can become so vivid that all you can think about is how to make it happen. That's when you know it's time to take a risk, enlist support, empower others, and boldly go towards the problem, knowing that you carry the solution. You will meet opposition. Still, it only serves as a launchpad to see God's provision and protection in ways you never have before. When we carry a vision, we never bear it alone. We carry it with the full promise and capacity of heaven, and what escaped accomplishment is suddenly accelerated because you dared to take a risk.

#

CHAPTER SIX
Focused Vision Directs Talent

::::::::::

I have a deep appreciation for talented people, but great talent doesn't make a great life. Great Talent steered by Great Vision is what makes life beautiful. In other words, Great Vision leads Great Talent.

Bernie was a legend because of his dreams, and what he created from them. There were other glass artisans that Bernie approached trying his best to convey the Great Vision that he'd seen. Those talented glassmakers all over the world could only make a second-rate replica of what Bernie saw. Was the sub-par work a lack of talent, or lack of vision? One thing's for sure; it's hard to make Great Beauty that you've never seen. Without Great Vision, Great Talent never lives up to its potential. It can only create beauty from an old story. Exceptional Talent is always dependent upon a personal encounter with Great Vision to produce Great Beauty.

Errantly, emphasizing talent alone accomplishes very little for our lives. Talent does not entitle us to the life of our dreams. Truthfully, our world is teeming with talented broken people. The world is also filled to the brim with successful people of average talent because Great Talent is not the only essential ingredient for success.

Great Talent may open doors, take us before royalty, and be our passport to distant lands. Still, it's a Great Vision that leads to real prosperity.

It's that God breathed future picture that takes Great Talent by the hand like a Kindergarten school kid and leads it to the best use. Great Talent will never keep us from perishing. Only Great Vision can do that. Without Great Vision to lead our Great Talent, we'll join the ranks of talented, broken people.

Some talented people can be unsuccessful in their relationships or make choices to their detriment. There are people who are wealthy in talent but impoverished in character. They don't flourish in their souls.

Consequently, we disqualify others who may not be as talented. We do not give them a second look, and we certainly don't think that they'll be the ones to lead us, advise us, direct us, or encourage us. In truth, talent can be common. There are a lot of talented singers, dancers, and waitresses in Hollywood. Everyone has some measure of it in some area or another. It may be undiscovered or underutilized, but it's there.

Then, there are those with Great Talent. Exceptional Talent is rare, and we appreciate the color that it adds to life. Great lives build on the foundation of Great Vision. It is possible to have a Great Talent and live a mediocre life. Many people do.

Consider Sampson and his Great Talent, killing a whole army of men single-handedly, ripping a lion to shreds, and escaping tightly bound ropes. No one would argue that Sampson had tremendous talent, but the quality of Sampson's life did not hinge on his Great Talent. The quality of Sampson's life depended upon him seeing the big picture. And, unfortunately, in his case, he caught hold of the vision a little too late.

On the other hand, consider Moses. I'm sure that Moses had talents, although scripture doesn't make this fact visible. We know he was raised as royalty and later became a shepherd. We know Moses failed Speech 101. He's not an interpreter of dreams, like Joseph. There's no theme song and fan club like David, and he lacks Solomon's wisdom. Moses' Great Talent is not apparent at first. We see it unfold encounter by encounter. Moses' Great Talent was his ability to recognize Great Vision. He saw God's vision for him, and he embraced it. Moses saw people free, and that singleness of vision propelled him into success.

Suddenly, murdering, stammering, stuttering Moses becomes the spokesman for two million people. He is the one who has an audience with the king and the King of Kings. He is the master negotiator God uses to broker freedom for a nation of people that had experienced centuries of enslavement. Moses is a history maker. Moses is the man. Not because of His Great Talent, but because of his Great Vision. He dared to see what God saw. He threatened to believe that he could make a difference.

By all means, be the talented individual that God created you to be. Use the Great Talents God has given you. But, don't allow your talent to lead you. Be led by Great Vision. Let Vision be the compass and use your ability to support the Vision that God has given you.

EVERY

==CREATED==

THING

:::::::HAS A:::::::

SPECIFIC

NOT A

RANDOM

FUNCTION

-Shenay Shumake

CHAPTER SEVEN
Divine Vision Carries Solutions

::::::::::

Great Vision always brings about Great Answers even when significant problems arise because of Great Vision.

Bernie's Great Vision was a critical factor in producing Great Beauty. When he lost his vision, it would seem that he lost the very ability that was needed to bring Great Beauty into his world and others. Bernie wondered why his door opened less frequently and had a surplus of his creations. He wondered what was so different now. But, when Bernie found his glasses, recapturing his vision changed the game. Bernie could see clearly with his glasses in place. Bernie's Great Vision leads to Great Answers. He recognized that what he thought was Great Beauty was nothing more than average. Bernie could now know what the problem had been all along: no vision = no beauty. With his glasses found Bernie could once again create the beauty that he craved.

Great Vision answered Bernie's problem, which was spurred on by Great Community. As a dreamer, he had what every dreamer needs, someone who believed in his dreams. Every dreamer is not always so blessed; some dreamers seem to have it more difficult because they live in a community of blindness or people with no vision, like Joseph. Being one of many siblings, he was the only one who dreamed. Unfortunately, it was his dreaming that got him in trouble.

"Now Joseph had a dream, and when he told it to his brothers, they hated him even more. He said to them, 'Hear this dream that I have dreamed: Behold, we were binding sheaves in the field, and behold, my sheaf arose and stood upright. And behold, your sheaves gathered around it and bowed down to my sheaf.' His brothers said to him, "Are you indeed to reign over us? So they hated him even more because of his dreams and his words." (Genesis 37:5-8)

There will always be people who don't see

your dream. People who within themselves cannot dream. Unfortunately, it can be the people that you see every day, which reminds you of how ordinary you are. When we share Great Vision with people who lack a vision of their own, it has the potential to alienate us.

"...They said to one another, "Here comes this dreamer. Come now, let us kill him and throw him into one of the pits. Then we will say that a fierce animal has devoured him, and we will see what will become of his dreams." (Genesis 37: 18-20)

The attacks of those who don't dream are less about you and more about your dreams. But the hopes that they try to steal become the dreams that they find themselves smack dab in the center of helping God bring to life.

The account of Joseph's life continues with Joseph being thrown into a pit by none other than his brothers. When travelers passed by on their way to Egypt, his brothers sell him into slavery. The boy who once was full of dreams is now a slave in a distant land. He is alienated from his family, and worst yet, his beloved father believes he is dead.

Egypt, however, is more than just a strange place; it is the backdrop for the fulfillment of Joseph's dreams. Joseph becomes the servant to the captain of the guard in Egypt. He lives the high life until he catches a case and ends up in prison. Still, in prison, God has great use for Joseph. He remains in jail two whole years before elevation and vindication. Joseph is eventually released from prison and rises to power in Egypt. He becomes the Secretary of Commerce.

God is now about to redeem the time in Joseph's life. The Great Problems that arose because of Great Vision get solved with Great answers. Many years have passed, and Joseph's family is still alive and well. And the famine in Canaan leads Joseph's brothers to partner in the fulfillment of Joseph's dreams. They are running smack dab into God's Great Vision for Joseph's life. The only way they can buy food is by seeing Joseph. Of course, just like in Joseph's dream, they greet him with a bow. Only they don't know it is Joseph until Joseph himself lets the cat out of the bag.

"I am your brother, Joseph, whom you sold into Egypt, And now do not be distressed or angry with yourselves because you sold me here, for God sent me before you to preserve life." (Genesis 45:4-5)

Joseph understood that his Great Vision caused significant problems. Still, in the end, it was a Great Vision that brought about Great Answers. The difficulties that Joseph faced, in the beginning, seemed to be problems he had to carry alone. But the Great Answers that Great Vision brought about were enough to extend—no to sustain his entire family. Joseph realized that the fulfillment of Great Vision had far-reaching implications.

"You shall dwell in the land of Goshen, and you shall be near me, you and your children, and your children's children, and your flocks, and your herds, and all that you have. There I will provide for you, so that you and your household, and all that you have do

not come to poverty." (Genesis 45:11)

When we see into our future, we know what will be. When we know what will be, it is not to the exclusion of problems. It just means that the issues never steal our focus because our destiny overshadows challenges.

There is no problem on the earth that God has not purposed someone to answer. Our challenge is catching hold of Great Vision so that we can bring resolution to the things that God has ordained for us to solve. Unfortunately, we spend more time worrying about the magnitude of the problem rather than the magnitude of God's Great Vision for us. When we are in the middle of our problems, Great Vision should be magnified, eclipsing what keeps us from Great Answers.

We cannot give significant problems the license to stop us from functioning at our highest self. To say that Joseph would have been overwhelmed is an understatement. Two years in what amounts to a dark, filthy ditch would jade even the eternal optimist.

Joseph, I'm sure, probably felt as if he had spent more than his fair share of time in ditches, none of which was a result of what he had done wrong. Even in that dark cavernous prison, Joseph knew that God had gifted him for a purpose; Joseph still dreamed dreams and brought understanding to the dreams of others. He still functioned at his highest self in the face of the bleakest circumstances. Joseph had a dream when he was young, and God's vision fulfilled is what sustained his family.

More than we need money in our hands, or jobs to go to every morning, more than we desperately need everything to go our way, we need a vision. Vision will sustain us when times are hard. Vision directs the resources that we have and propagates them so that we are not in short supply.

PURPOSE
IS ----------
natural
intentional
----------AND
POWERFUL

-Shenay Shumake

CHAPTER EIGHT
Successful Vision Requires Consistency

::::::::::

There cannot be the realization of Great Vision and the creation of Great Beauty without the rigor of Great Discipline.

We've all heard the popular definition of insanity. "Insanity is doing the same thing over and over again and expecting different results." Sometimes that definition is correct. However, there are rare times, appointed seasons, when the same thing that you've always done or the same thing that has always happened suddenly yields a different result. Malcolm Gladwell calls it, "The Tipping Point." The truth is that insane repetition is just what you need to bring Great Beauty to your life. Every Great Vision demands Great Discipline.

Bernie was the best of the best because of what he saw and what he did with what he saw. With every Great Dream that he dreamed, he took Great Action. Bernie began each day with a prayer of praise and thanksgiving. He got dressed and prepared breakfast. Then, he headed off to his workroom. These were Bernie's daily habits or Bernie's morning rituals. Bernie's simple daily habits formed the foundation of his Great Action, which allowed him to create Great Beauty. These certainly don't seem like Great Actions. But actions don't fall into the high category because they are heroic feats. Works become Great Actions because they lead us steadily and consistently toward the realization of our dreams.

Great Action is not always the monumental steps that we take in fulfilling our dreams. Great Action is any action that will consistently lead us in the direction of fulfillment of Great Vision. There is a lot to be said for having a daily routine.

A daily routine is a systematic way that we take bites out of big elephants. The lack of a daily routine can be the little foxes that spoil our vine. Any action that we take consistently will yield a result. Whether we always neglect our dreams, or whether we march toward them with purpose in every step, we will get a result. We must order our consistent actions so that they become the Great Action that helps us fulfill Great Vision. Ordering our efforts requires Great Discipline, and fulfilling Great Vision demands it.

All our actions toward Great Vision do not have to be grand events. To only celebrate the big things and not appreciate the small things that we can do daily, will create a lack of appreciation for every action. The truth is, no action is neutral. We are either led closer to our dreams in small or large steps or growing further distant by the same degree. One single grand Great Action serves only the purpose of motivating us toward more action. It is the small, consistent habits of our daily routine that stack up to be the Great Action that propels us to accomplish Great Vision. We must create for ourselves a "normal."

Your "normal" is the Great Discipline that Great Vision demands. Sometimes by doing the unexpected, we can achieve a Great Vision. Great Vision requires that we discover what key activities will propel us toward achievement and that we practice those key activities routinely. Great Vision demands this kind of Great Discipline. While growing in daily disciplines, we'll do ordinary things with unprecedented results.

"Normal" is plainly dressed when we hold it up against the backdrop of the vivid dreams that we've been dreaming. That's because our dreams have produced passion in us, and we are motivated to do unconventional things. We think of ways to be smart and innovative as we work to fulfill our dreams. We want secrets to share and keys that unlock the mystery of how we've accomplished heroic feats. "Normal" is not the place we should be looking for these things.

As plain as "normal" is. "Normal" is not easy. "Normal" like great vision requires Great Discipline. Normal is the pace that you can sustain and what you can accomplish repeatedly. Your "normal" requires focus. Your "normal" involves energy and consistency. Your "normal" requires that you see your daily habits as critical to the fulfillment of Great Vision.

God had a Great Vision for the Children of Israel led by Joshua. He would give them the great double-walled city of Jericho. Jericho's outer wall was six feet thick and the inner wall, twelve feet thick. The walls of Jericho were so thick that often, the guards would line their chariots side-by-side, and they would race around the perimeter of the inner wall. To besiege a city like Jericho, one would think that you'd need a battering ram, a stick of dynamite, or an army three times the size of Jericho. No one would think that a lap around that great city every day for six days and then seven times on the last, coupled with a loud shout, would be all that was required to bring those walls down, but that's exactly what happened.

"So the people shouted, and priests blew the trumpets; and when the people heard the sound of the

trumpet, the people shouted with a great shout and the wall fell flat, so that the people went up into the city, every man straight ahead, and they took the city." (Joshua 6:20)

The victory over Jericho for the children of Israel did not lie in their power or ability. The victory over Jericho did not lie in their resources. What sealed the victory for the children of Israel was that they did what God said repeatedly. It was obedience to God carried out through their extreme discipline. It was their "norm" for the next seven days.

They woke up, assembled, blew the shofar, left camp, and walked the circumference of Jericho in complete silence. Then they blew the shofar again and went back to camp. They did the same thing every day for six days. It was a silent parade. No bells and whistles were accompanying this miracle, no standing still and watching the Red Sea as walls of water welled up on either side and dry ground appeared. There was no burning bush, or sudden rain, no ram in the forest, no floating ax heads. Just get up, get in line, shut up, blow the trumpet, and walk.

This to-do list is simple, and it seems boring. Simple, seemingly stupid instructions from the God who brings bread from the sky, water out of a rock, and talks in a cloud. Now here they were exercising Great Discipline and wondering how God would give them this city. They were doing what God had asked them to do, the kinds of things they had always done, every day for the next seven days, nothing more and nothing less, and those walls were pushed down because of it.

What walls need to be pushed down in your life? What if your family's generational promise is wrapped up in your daily obedience? What if something that is well within your ability to accomplish, something you may even take for granted, is the tool that God uses to measure your obedience to Him and the degree to which you marvel at His power.

If we think that God always requires us to leave our family, scale enemy walls or walk on water, we don't know God. He is Sovereign. He reserves the right to change the method. He only asks of us as Eugene Peterson puts it, "long obedience in the same direction." God knows how to show up in the ordinary. If we can walk in Great Obedience, merely exercising the Great Discipline that Great Vision demands, we could set the stage for exceptional results.

To accomplish Great Vision, we must exercise our ability to do the things that are within our capacity. We routinely and thoroughly act, drawing us closer to the fulfillment of a Great Vision and the creation of Great Beauty.

CHAPTER NINE
Great Vision Outlives Great Lives

::::::::::

Long after Bernie has reached the end of his life's spectrum, his glass will still sit on the shelves of collectors around the world. Generations to come will appreciate the Great Beauty that Bernardo Salomon offered, perfect renderings of his Great Visions.

Every eternal thing begins with Great Vision. If we are to leave a legacy, we must know that Great Beauty born of Great Vision transcends lifetimes.

It may not take a lifetime to create Great Beauty, but Great Beauty is admired for ages. Michelangelo took only four years to conceive and paint the Sistine Chapel. He died at the age of 88 and sculpted and painted much of his life. Today, we still marvel at his work and how he is one of the greatest artists that ever lived.

Michelangelo was a great artist but was an even greater visionary. He started with the same materials that any other artist would begin a masterpiece with. Still, every artistic undertaking started with the end in mind. Michelangelo saw of every blank canvas and every piece of stone that could be. Sculpting, he once said, "... every block of stone has a statue inside of it, and it is the task of the sculptor to discover it." What he discovered in blocks of stone, was a Great Beauty that he offered. While others saw just stone, he saw the future picture of what it will be. Centuries later, his carefully sculpted visions still display Great Beauty. His visions live on.

Every God-breathed vision mimics the beauty and picture of a God who is eternal. When we discover Great Vision, we uncover just a fraction of a future image of Great Beauty. Every person and all of creation is a mere snapshot bearing in the smallest sense a bit of God's beauty. And every created thing that has had incalculable value to man's existence has been a polaroid of God's Great Beauty. And has its origin in the heart and mind of the great visionary. We may not know the names of great visionaries, but we know their work. Because of who we are, what we see, and what we offer, we are beautiful little pieces of a sizeable eternal puzzle that points to the glory and splendor of God. And what we see through our God-given scope is the grand vision that is always eternally beautiful. Jesus epitomizes the eternal concept and eternal beauty.

Jesus Christ is an eternally beautiful visionary. Two thousand years after he walked the earth, still we preach his vision that he came to offer life abundantly. Jesus saw people no longer violated, dead, and annihilated. He saw people living superfluous, abundant in quantity, and quality kind of life. His message of abundant living transcended shifts in geographical boundaries, technological advances, the dawning of ages, and the collapse and rise of governments. Great men from then to today say this of Jesus.

- **Augustine of Hippo in 400 AD** said of Jesus, "I have read in Plato and Cicero sayings that are very wise and very beautiful; but I never read in either of them: *"Come unto me all ye that labor and are heavy laden."*

- "Let every student be plainly instructed and earnestly pressed to consider well, the main end of his life and studies is, to know God and Jesus Christ, which is eternal life, (John 17:3); and therefore to lay Jesus Christ as the only foundation of all sound knowledge and learning. And seeing the Lord only giveth wisdom, let everyone seriously set himself by prayer in secret to seek it of him (Proverbs 2:3)." — **From the first Harvard University Student Handbook**

- **Napoleon Bonaparte, French General, Politician, and Emperor** said of Jesus, "I know men, and I tell you that Jesus Christ is no mere man. Between Him and every other person in the world, there is no possible term of comparison. Alexander, Caesar,

Charlemagne, and I founded empires; but what foundation did we rest the creations of our genius? Upon force. Jesus Christ founded an empire upon love, and at this hour, millions of men would die for Him."

- "For thirty-five years of my life, I was, in the proper acceptation of the word, nihilist, a man who believed in nothing. Five years ago, my faith came to me. I believed in the doctrine of Jesus Christ, and my whole life underwent a sudden transformation. Life and death ceased to be evil. Instead of despair, I tasted joy and happiness that death could not take away." — **Leo Tolstoy, the great genius of Russian letters**

- "Jesus Christ was an extremist for love, truth, and goodness." — **Martin Luther King Jr., American civil rights leader**

- "It is as if God the Father is saying to us:

"Since I have told you everything in My Word, Who is My Son, I have no other words that can at present say anything or reveal anything to you beyond this. Fix your eyes on Him alone, for in Him, I have told you all, revealed all, and in Him, you will find more than you desire or ask. If you fix your eyes on Him, you will find everything, for He is My whole word and My reply, He is My whole vision and My whole revelation." **Anthony M. Coniaris – Greek Orthodox Pastor**

Long after we are gone, Christ's vision will live. No one else will ever touch the world with such Great Beauty. Jesus Christ's vision is incomparably great.

The greatness of Christ's vision should inspire as we follow the footsteps of God Himself. Seeing like Him, we can offer an eternally beautiful vision that blesses future generations.

CHAPTER TEN
My Final Thoughts

:::::::::

The world always has room for Great Vision, because deep down inside of every human being, God has created a craving for Great Beauty. Offering Great Beauty helps us to satisfy the need for Great Beauty in others and satisfies our desire for significance.

Perhaps the best thing about Great Vision is that it knows no age demographics. It's never too late to begin to see it, and it's never too early to ink your dreams. Great Vision weaves its way into the conversation that we have with school children in the purest form of the question, "What do you want to be when you grow up?" It becomes our interrogation when we converse with the old, "Did you do everything that you saw yourself doing when you were young?" When we are young and old our hearts and minds turn to thoughts about meaning. Great Vision can be a constant companion, from the moment we are born until we breathe our last.

Grand Vision is also not exclusive. It transcends socio-economic barriers, ethnic categories, and political preferences. It is a faithful companion to those that are faithful to it. It can be an anchor when life is drifting, or a lifeboat when you feel you will drown in the sea. During your life, you can't always predict the shape that it takes, but the result will still spur hope.

Vision has incalculable value. Don't ignore your vibrant dreams. Know your inklings, ideas, and notions are significant clues to Great Vision and the best use of your life. And, be convinced that you can see the future. The picture of it can impassion you. The world will know the impact of what you see and will benefit from what you do with what you see. Above all, understand that the "glass" that you make can bring glory to God, serve humanity, and leave an undeniable legacy for future generations.

ABOUT THE AUTHOR

:::::::::

With a heart on fire, Shenay Shumake lights up souls with truth, power, and hope. Her blend of grace and grit moves audiences from comfort to action.

When Shenay was a child, her life was stained by the tragic murder of her father and she's not afraid to spill the tea about what happens to a girl when she doesn't see a father in the world. Her message of being deeply loved and wildly courageous paints the picture of what restoration looks like and how to live a fuller, deeper, richer and more satisfying life-no matter who you are or where you're from.

As a coach and leader, she inspires men and women to hit the reset button and get after it! She loves seeing people be who they were created to be. As the founder and hosts of Grow Workshops® she reminds women that they, "are born to be a radiant and gorgeous flower who blooms in the light of the Son."

No matter what she's doing her deepest desire is to partner with the Holy Spirit to convey biblical truths that help people uncover their identity, pursue purpose with passion and live out their true potential in Jesus.

Shenay hails from the "D" - Detroit, Michigan where she loves, lives, and leads Life Changer's International Ministries alongside her husband, "Flette", the love of her life for two and a half decades. She is the proud mama bear to four adult children Nia, Micah, Caleb, and Zoe and she is "Mama Nay" to her darling grandson, Judah.

APPENDIX

[1]. Eldredge, John. Captivating: Unveiling the Mystery of a Woman's Soul, Keepsake Edition. Nashville, TN: Thomas Nelson, 2007.

[2] Richards, Norman. *Helen Keller*. Chicago: Children's Press, 1968.

[3] Michael Hyatt. "Why Vision Is More Important Than Strategy." Michael Hyatt, August 12, 2012. https://michaelhyatt.com/why-vision-is-more-important-than-strategy/.

[4] Stanley, Andy. Visioneering - God's Blueprint for Developing and Maintaining Vision. Multnomah Press, 2005.

www.ingramcontent.com/pod-product-compliance
Lightning Source LLC
LaVergne TN
LVHW021542080426
835509LV00019B/2787